My Little Golden

GEORGE WASHINGTON

by Lori Haskins Houran

illustrated by Viviana Garofoli

The editors would like to thank Mary V. Thompson, Research Historian,
The Fred W. Smith National Library for the Study of George Washington,
for her assistance in the preparation of this book.

A GOLDEN BOOK • NEW YORK

randomhousekids.com
Educators and librarians, for a variety of teaching tools, visit us at
RHTeachersLibrarians.com
Library of Congress Control Number: 2015944892
ISBN 978-1-101-93969-7 (trade) — ISBN 978-1-101-93970-3 (ebook)
Printed in the United States of America
10 9 8 7 6 5 4 3 2

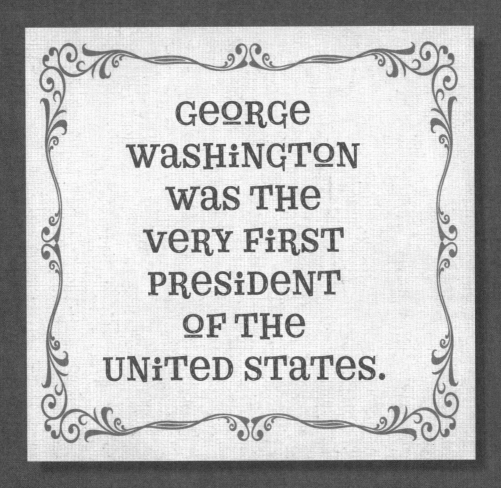

GEORGE
WASHINGTON
WAS THE
VERY FIRST
PRESIDENT
OF THE
UNITED STATES.

Growing up, George never dreamed he would be president. America wasn't even a country yet!

America was just thirteen pieces of land, called colonies, that belonged to the country of England.

George lived in the colony of Virginia, on his family's farm.

He was a tall, quiet boy. He didn't mind studying or doing chores.

But whenever he could, George slipped
outdoors. He loved to fish in the river, hunt in
the woods, and ride horseback over the rolling
green hills.

When George turned twenty, he joined the army. England needed soldiers. Another country, France, was trying to take over some land near the colonies.

George was a good soldier—brave and smart. He was lucky, too. In one battle, four bullets whizzed through his cloak, but George was not hurt!

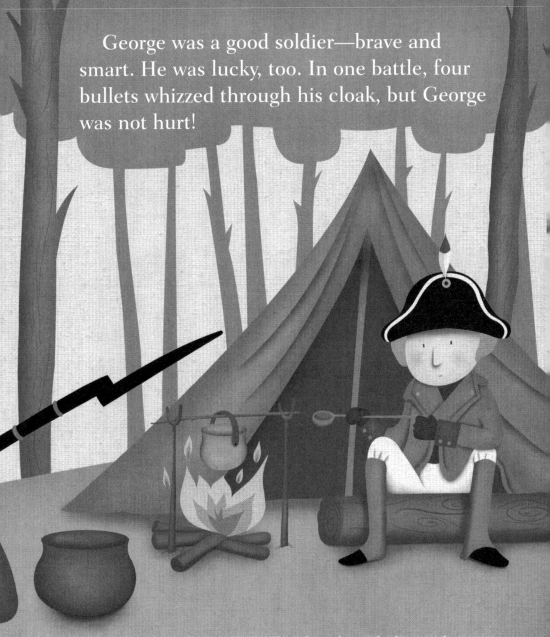

Working together, England and the colonies beat France.

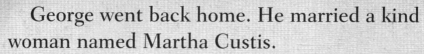

George went back home. He married a kind woman named Martha Custis.

George was happy. He had his own farm now, Mount Vernon, where he could fish and hunt and ride.

But he didn't get to stay home for long.

Trouble was brewing. The colonies didn't like the way England was treating them. They wanted to break off and form their own country. But the king of England said no.

If the colonies wanted freedom, they would have to fight for it.

People remembered how well George had fought against France. They asked him to lead a new war—this time against England.

George agreed to become America's top general. He took charge of the entire army!

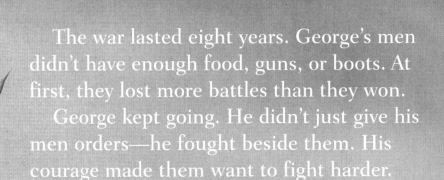

The war lasted eight years. George's men
didn't have enough food, guns, or boots. At
first, they lost more battles than they won.

George kept going. He didn't just give his
men orders—he fought beside them. His
courage made them want to fight harder.

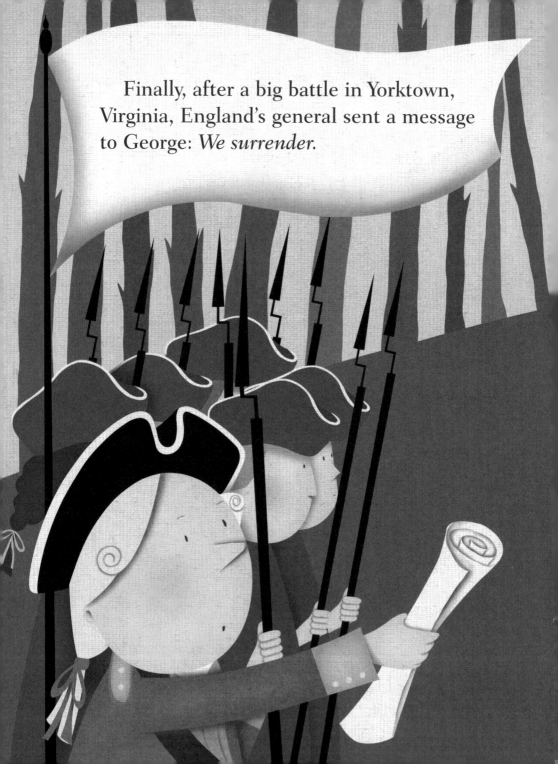

Finally, after a big battle in Yorktown, Virginia, England's general sent a message to George: *We surrender.*

The war was over. America was free!
No longer would the colonists be ruled by
the king of a faraway country.

The thirteen colonies became the first
states. These states formed a brand-new
country: the United States of America.

Someone had to lead the country. Someone brave and smart. Someone who knew how to take charge.

An election was held to choose the first president.

George won every vote!

George got right to work.

He helped the states join together peacefully.

He set up a new government with new laws, and new American money.

He even chose the spot where the White House would be built!

After eight years, George looked around.
He saw that America was growing into a
fine, strong nation.

It was time, George decided, to let
someone else be president.

George went back to Mount Vernon with Martha. It was good to be home!

He took care of his farm. He welcomed visitors—lots of visitors. Everyone wanted to meet the most famous man in America! George didn't mind.

But whenever he could, George slipped outdoors . . .

. . . to fish in the river, hunt in the woods,
and ride horseback over the rolling green hills.

REMEMBERING GEORGE

We honor our first president in many ways.
His picture is on our dollar bill and our
quarter. It has been on many stamps.

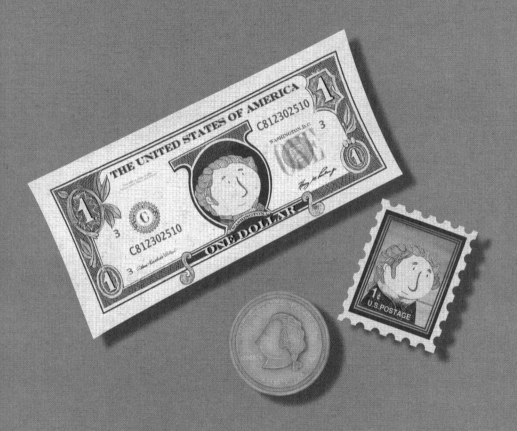

Our capital, where the president lives today,
is named for him: Washington, D.C. And that's
where the Washington Monument stands.

His face was carved into a mountain called Mount Rushmore, alongside other favorite presidents.

And every year, on the third Monday in February, we celebrate his birthday.

HAPPY BiRTHDAY, GEORGE!